"If you think the Christmas story is a fairy tale for kids, I strongly recommend you read this book!"

RUSSELL COWBURN, Professor of Experimental Physics, Cambridge University

"Rebecca McLaughlin has quickly become one of my favorite Christian apologists. If you are looking for a good book to give to an unbelieving friend at Christmas or are searching for answers yourself, this book will be a welcome friend."

LIGON DUNCAN, Chancellor and CEO, Reformed Theological Seminary

"So many people have been shaken by the COVID pandemic; we're fragile, not in control, often lonely or angry, and longing for a God to believe in. But we have to know it's true, and that is why Rebecca McLaughlin's little Christmas book *Is Christmas Unbelievable?* is so timely. She tells the story of Christmas, gives the facts that ground it in history, defends the miraculous, and explains the relevance of it all."

RICO TICE, Founder, Christianity Explored Ministries

"With lucid brevity and timely insight, Rebecca McLaughlin's book wisely anticipates both the cognitive and emotional questions in the mind and heart of the skeptic. This is exactly the kind of cultural apologetics we need for today--one that is wise and winsome. Take up, read and then share."

JULIUS J. KIM, PhD, President, The Gospel Coalition

"What a gift! This little book shows us that rational grown-ups don't need to stop believing in Christmas. It's the perfect thing to send with a Christmas card."

PETER J. WILLIAMS, Author, *Can We Trust the Gospels?*

REBECCA McLAUGHLIN

IS CHRISTMAS

UNBELIEVABLE?

thegoodbook
COMPANY

For Carrie... because
"even atheists love a manger scene"!

Is Christmas Unbelievable?
© Rebecca McLaughlin, 2021

Published by
The Good Book Company

thegoodbook.com | thegoodbook.co.uk
thegoodbook.com.au | thegoodbook.co.nz | thegoodbook.co.in

ISBN: 9781784986407 | Printed in India

Design by André Parker

Contents

Introduction

Dear Santa. Thank you for the dolls and pencils and the fish. It's Easter now, so I hope I didn't wake you, but honest, it is an emergency. There is a crack in my wall. Aunt Shie says it's just an ordinary crack, but I know it's not because at night there's voices. So please, PLEASE, can you send someone to fix it?

A seven-year-old (Amy Pond) is kneeling by her bed, praying to Santa, when the iconic sci-fi hero Doctor Who crash-lands his time-and-spaceship in her garden. If you're not familiar with Doctor Who, the Doctor is a human-looking alien with two hearts and a superhuman mind. He's hundreds of years old, and he travels through time and space making friends and saving worlds. Conveniently (both for the Doctor and for the show), instead of dying, he regenerates. In this episode, he's just regenerated into a new body. He eats half the food in Amy's house, but he doesn't fix the scary crack in her wall. He tells her it's a crack in the skin of the universe, and then he goes away, promising he'll come back in five minutes.

But he doesn't.

Amy draws pictures of the "raggedy Doctor" to keep him fresh in her mind. She grows up clinging to the idea that the hero who dropped from the sky to save her world when she was a kid was actually real.

I don't know how you think about the Christmas story. Perhaps you believed it at Amy's age. But now the story of the infant Son of God, cradled in a manger but born to save the world, sounds about as far-fetched as Doctor Who. Messenger angels. A virgin giving birth. A guiding star. Can anyone too old to believe in Santa really be expected to believe such things?

This book will answer, "Yes." It will look at four questions we should all ask about the story of Jesus' birth, and it will show that—while even some kids may be skeptical—some of the most respected scholars in the world believe the Christmas story to be true. What's more, it will suggest that if God really did become human just over 2,000 years ago, that's really good news for us here now. Because—like Amy Pond—we have an emergency.

December brings a heavenly host of emotions. I don't know if you relish Christmas or if you dread it, if you're full of joy and love or if you feel alone and lost. Maybe you're living your dreams. Or maybe life isn't quite turning out the way you'd hoped when you were seven.

Perhaps you feel no need of a Savior. Perhaps, if you're honest, you're ready to try anything.

However you're feeling right now, I hope this little book will help you think a little more about the man who landed in our world 2,000 years ago. I hope it will persuade you that he's more important than you thought. And I hope it will make you wonder if his unbelievable claim that he'd come to save the world— and you and me—from an emergency more serious than Amy Pond's might just be true.

CHAPTER 1

Was Jesus Even a Real Person?

"**I** told all my friends that Santa isn't real, but Jesus is!"

When my five-year-old came home with this news, her teacher had already told me (with concern) that she'd been directing other kids to act out the Christmas story. "You're Mary. You're Joseph. You're the angel." I was torn between admiring her gumption and dreading awkward conversations with other parents!

For many kids, Santa is the real star of Christmas. It's mostly the presents. But it's also that sense of magic—the idea that someone with supernatural powers might just be listening to them. Amy Pond is not the only child ever to have prayed to Santa.

Is believing in Jesus just as naïve?

Plenty of people would answer, *Yes!* In fact, one survey in 2015 found that 40% of adults in the UK didn't think that Jesus was even a real person, or weren't sure.[1] 22%

thought he was "a mythical or fictional character." So, before we look at the specifics of Jesus' birth, we need to ask if he was born at all.

Did Jesus Even Exist?

In 2012, New Testament scholar Bart Ehrman wrote a book on this question: *Did Jesus Exist? The Historical Argument for Jesus of Nazareth.* Ehrman doesn't believe in God. In fact, he's made a fortune writing books that question the historic Christian faith. But as Ehrman explains, "The reality is that whatever else you may think about Jesus, he certainly did exist."[2] Ehrman says this view "is held by virtually every expert on the planet."[3] Rather than it being naïve to believe that Jesus walked the earth 2,000 years ago, it's actually naïve not to.

So, what evidence leads all these experts to conclude that Jesus did exist? The richest sources we have for Jesus' life are the four biographies that we find in the New Testament part of the Bible: the so-called "Gospels" of Matthew, Mark, Luke, and John. Ehrman calls these Gospels "the oldest and best sources we have for knowing about the life of Jesus," and says this is "the view of all serious historians of antiquity of every kind, from committed evangelical Christians to hardcore atheists."[4] We'll look at the Gospel accounts of Jesus' birth in a bit. But even if we lay the Gospels aside entirely, multiple ancient documents by non-Christian authors also contain references to Jesus Christ. These snatches of information are often given in passing in pieces of writing mostly concerned with other things. Nonetheless, from these non-biblical sources we can still piece together the basics of Jesus' life and death.

One such reference to Jesus is in a text written by the Jewish historian Josephus in around AD 93. Josephus reports that in AD 62 (about three decades after Jesus' death) the Jewish high priest "had a man named James, the brother of Jesus who was called the Christ, and certain others" stoned (i.e. executed).5 This fits with what the Bible says. At this point in history, God's people (the Jews) were living under oppressive Roman rule. But God had promised to send a special King—the "Christ"—to rescue them. In the Gospels, Jesus claimed to be that Christ. The New Testament also identifies James as Jesus' brother and as a leader in the early church.[6] The Christians were seen as heretics by the Jewish authorities, so James getting executed by stoning makes sense.

We find another reference to Jesus Christ in an early 2nd-century document by the Roman historian Cornelius Tacitus. Tacitus reports how the Emperor Nero blamed the Great Fire of Rome of AD 64 on "a class of men, loathed for their vices, whom the crowd called *Chrestians*" (another spelling of Christians). Tacitus goes on to explain who these Christians were:

> *"Christus, the founder of the name, had undergone the death penalty in the reign of Tiberius, by*

sentence of the procurator Pontius Pilatus, and the
pernicious superstition was checked for a moment,
only to break out once more, not merely in Judea,
the home of the disease, but in [Rome] itself, where
all things horrible or shameful in the world collect
and become fashionable."[7]

Tacitus was no fan of the Christians! But his account confirms what the Gospels claim: that Jesus who was called Christ was executed during the reign of the Emperor Tiberius and under the authority of Pontius Pilate, who was governor of Judea from AD 26 to 36.

By the early 2nd century, Christianity had become a real Roman headache. Pliny the Younger (a Roman governor in Turkey from around 109-111) wrote a letter to the emperor, asking for advice on persecuting Christians. Pliny required those suspected of being Christians to worship Roman gods, offer adoration to a statue of the emperor, and curse Christ. He knew real Christians wouldn't do these things. Some who confessed to having previously been Christians said they had been in the habit of meeting early in the morning on a certain day of the week and singing "a hymn to Christ as to a god."[8] Unlike most of their religious contemporaries, Christians saw Jesus not just as one god to be worshiped among many, but rather as the one true God. Worshiping Jesus meant not worshiping anyone else.

To find out more about Christianity, Pliny tortured "two female slaves, who were called deaconesses."[9] His picks were representative of the type of people who made up the early church; Christianity seems to have been particularly popular among women and slaves. In fact, the 2nd-century Greek philosopher Celsus quipped that Christians "want and are able to convince only the foolish, dishonorable and stupid, only slaves, women, and little children."[10] Pliny, however, is clear that the "contagious superstition" of Christianity had spread to people "of all ages and ranks and of both sexes."[11]

These three early texts give us evidence from outside the Bible that Jesus was a Jewish leader in the early 1st century, that he claimed to be the Christ, that he was executed by the Romans between AD 26 and 36, and that he was subsequently worshiped by his followers as God.

At this point, you may be thinking, "Ok, I get that Jesus was a real person, who claimed to be the Christ and was executed by the Romans. But the Bible asks us to believe much more than that." You're right! Like the young Amy Pond drawing pictures of her "raggedy Doctor" while everybody thought she was delusional, believing in the Christmas story *does* mean believing some truly unbelievable things—things that Greek philosophers thought only uneducated slaves, women, and children would buy! We'll get to some of those in chapter 3.

But not everything you may have heard about Christmas comes from the Bible. Over time, Christmas has grown to include all sorts of extra details in our popular imagination—like the idea that Jesus was born in the bleak midwinter, that it was snowing at the time, or that his nativity involved a little donkey, a grumpy innkeeper, a stable, and a little drummer boy. (*Pa rum-pum-pum pum.*) None of this is in the Gospels. So, what *do* the Gospels say?

What Is the Christmas Story?

Matthew's and Luke's Gospels introduce us to Mary: a young Jewish woman, living in 1st-century Judea. Mary was betrothed (a legally binding form of engagement) to a man called Joseph. But, as Matthew euphemistically puts it, "Before they came together she was found to be with child from the Holy Spirit" (Matthew 1:18*). Luke tells us that Mary was forewarned of this by an angel called Gabriel. Gabriel told Mary to call her son Jesus and said he was the promised King, who would reign over God's people forever (Luke 1:26-38). Mary was understandably surprised—both by the angel and by his message! But she believed what Gabriel said and went on to voice one of the greatest poems of praise to God in the whole Bible (Luke 1:46-55)!

Matthew tells the story from Joseph's perspective. When he found out Mary was pregnant, Joseph assumed she'd cheated on him. But then Joseph met an angel in a dream, who told him the baby's father was God himself.

---

* That is, the Gospel of Matthew, chapter 1, verse 18.

The angel told Joseph to call the baby Jesus (which means "God is salvation") and explained, "For he will save his people from their sins" (Matthew 1:21).

This is a surprising twist.

The 1st-century Jews were waiting for someone to save them from the Romans. But the angel's words suggested they had a bigger problem. In *Doctor Who*, the crack in Amy's bedroom wall turned out to be a crack in the universe itself—a crack that was gnawing away at her family, her city, and her world. And according to the Bible, there's a crack in our universe too—a crack that cuts us off from God and from each other, a crack that passes right through every human heart: a terrible crack called sin. According to the angel, this baby had come to save his people *from their sins*. He was the prophesied "Immanuel," which means "God with us"—in the person of Jesus, God himself came to earth to make it possible for his people to be *with* him again (Matthew 1:22-23). This was Jesus' mission: to bring sinful people back into God's embrace.

Unlike the virgin birth of *Star Wars* character Anakin Skywalker, the Gospels don't set Jesus' birth long, long ago in a galaxy far, far away. They pin it to an actual time and place. This is no mythological account. But the precise dating is also not straightforward. Matthew and Luke both talk about Jesus being born during the reign of King Herod, who died in 4 BC. But Luke also claims that while Mary was pregnant, Joseph had to report to his hometown—Bethlehem—to be registered as part of "the first registration when Quirinius was governor of Syria" (Luke 2:2). Based on the writings of the Jewish historian Josephus, many scholars date the census under Quirinius to AD 6—roughly ten years after Herod's death. Some critics say this means we can discount the Gospels as historical documents. Jesus being born in Bethlehem was significant, as Israel's archetypal king—King David—had been born in Bethlehem too. So (the argument goes), Luke must have invented the census to get Mary and Joseph to Bethlehem for the birth.

But it's not so simple. You see, by all the usual tests for historical documents, the Gospels stand up very well. We'll look at this more in the next chapter, but in ancient historical terms, they were written very soon after the events they describe, and the manuscript evidence we have for the Gospels is extraordinarily good by comparison with other documents that we take to be historical.[12] What's more, the Gospel writers show remarkable depth of local knowledge about the region and time in which Jesus lived.[13] Scholars have proposed various potential solutions to the apparent discrepancy between what Luke and Josephus each say about the census. One is that Luke was right, and that Josephus was unaware of an earlier census.[14] And when you think about it, if Luke had wanted to invent a reason to get Mary and Joseph to Bethlehem for the birth, he could have claimed something much less problematic than a census: like Joseph's favorite uncle inviting them to stay! So, we can't reasonably dismiss Luke's Gospel just because of this challenge.

Once they got to Bethlehem, Mary and Joseph didn't head to the best hotel in town, as would befit the birth of a King. Instead, Luke tells us that there was "no place for them in the inn," so Jesus ended up sleeping in a manger: an animal feeding trough (Luke 2:7). This doesn't have to mean he was born in a stable. It was not uncommon for village houses at that time to feature mangers. But the manger detail does show us that Jesus wasn't born into wealth and privilege: quite the reverse. Luke also tells us that an angel appeared to some local shepherds (who would have been seen as riffraff in that culture) to tell them that the Christ had been born and where to find him: in the afore-mentioned manger (Luke 2:8-20).

Matthew introduces more impressive visitors. Wise men from the east had been led by a star to Jerusalem. Rather tactlessly, they asked the then current Roman-sanctioned king of the Jews—King Herod—"Where is he who has been born king of the Jews? For we saw his star when it rose and have come to worship him" (Matthew 2:2). Herod was troubled and asked the leading Jewish theologians where the Christ was meant to be born. They said Bethlehem. So, Herod dispatched these wise men to find Jesus, claiming that he wanted to worship him as well. (In fact, Herod wanted to kill Jesus; he was quite happy with the existing king of the Jews, thank you very much!) The star went before the wise men, "until it came to rest over the place where the child was" (Matthew 2:9). When they found Jesus, they fell down and worshiped him, and they offered him gifts of gold, frankincense, and myrrh (Matthew 2:11). These three gifts led to the later Christmas tradition of calling these wise men "three kings." That's not what the Bible says. But Matthew does imply that these stargazers were outsiders in Israel. Jesus hadn't come only for the Jewish people. He was worshiped by foreigners from the first.

There's something very touching about this story of a divine child lying in a manger, heralded by angels and hated by rulers, but worshiped by both rich and poor, by fellow Jews and foreigners, by stargazing scholars and uneducated shepherds. It's a lovely Yuletide tale for the kids—so long as you stop before Herod has all the boys under two years old in the region killed! But it's also a story rooted in history.

So, despite being only five, my daughter wasn't naïve to tell her friends that Santa isn't real but that Jesus is. Even if we exclude the evidence of the Gospels, Jesus was undoubtedly a real person in history, and his birth, life, death, and claimed resurrection undeniably changed the world.

CHAPTER 2

Can We Take the Gospels Seriously?

In *Harry Potter and the Half Blood Prince*, Professor Dumbledore summons Harry to a series of lessons in his office. Dumbledore has been gathering evidence about the life of the evil Lord Voldemort. He's extracted memories from various sources (ranging from house elves to his own brain), and with the help of his magical "pensieve", Dumbledore invites Harry to plunge into other people's pasts. One memory is from 60 years ago. Two have been drawn from people shortly before they died. One has been tampered with, so Dumbledore sends Harry to retrieve the true original. The details of Voldemort's life—his parentage, his words, his deeds, even the prophesies concerning him—are all vital information.

At the beginning of his Gospel, Luke tells us how he got his intel about Jesus. Like Dumbledore, he's gathered information from "those who from the beginning were eyewitnesses" (Luke 1:2). John's Gospel—the last to be written down—makes a yet bolder claim: that it is Jesus' disciple John's own eyewitness testimony (John 21:24).

But could this really be true? Weren't the Gospels written much too long after the events they describe to be believable? Can we take them seriously as sources on Jesus' birth, life, and death?

Are the Gospels like the Telephone Game?

According to the famous atheist Richard Dawkins, "Everything that is in the gospels suffered from decades of word-of-mouth retelling, Chinese-Whispery distortion and exaggeration before those four texts were finally written down."[15] Growing up in England, I sometimes played a game known as "Chinese Whispers." As so often is the case with racist expressions, I didn't realize at the time that there were racist overtones to this term. Thankfully, in America (where I now live) it's known as the Telephone Game. A bunch of kids sit in a circle. The first child whispers a message to their neighbor, who whispers it to the next child, and so on. The last kid says out loud the message they heard and everyone laughs at how much it has changed. Both Richard Dawkins and Bart Ehrman use this game as an analogy for how the Gospels came to be. So, is this a fair comparison?

Most scholars think that Mark's Gospel was the first to be written, about 35 to 45 years after Jesus' death.

Before that time, the stories about Jesus were passed on by word of mouth. But unlike in the Telephone Game, they were not whispered along a single chain. They were proclaimed in synagogues and market-places and from house to house. And rather than depending on a single source (like the first child), there were thousands of witnesses to Jesus' preaching and miracles. Large crowds gathered to hear him teach, and a smaller band of disciples traveled with him for several years. Twelve of these disciples (known as "apostles") were specially chosen to pass on what Jesus taught. Like the child who starts the telephone game, they knew first-hand what Jesus said and did. If there was ever any doubt as the message spread, they could be consulted.

In his ground-breaking book, *Jesus and the Eyewitnesses*, world-class New Testament scholar Richard Bauckham argues that the Gospels were written down when they were because the original eyewitnesses were starting to die out. Bauckham shows that specific people are named in the Gospels to flag them as eyewitness sources. It was a way of saying, "If you don't believe me, ask Mary Magdalene—she saw it with her own eyes!" In the case of John's Gospel, Bauckham argues that it was indeed written by John himself.[16] If this is true, John's Gospel isn't like the moment in the Telephone Game when the last child says what they think they heard. It's like the moment when the first child reports what the original message actually was. But could people *really* remember what they'd seen and heard from Jesus 35, 40 or even 60 years later?

Wasn't the Time Lag Just Too Long?

My older brother was born on Christmas Eve. My mum remembers the details of his birth. She also remembers how unimpressed she was when my dad hired a flute trio to play her music when she brought the baby home! (My dad meant well, but, believe me, if your wife has just given birth, she doesn't want to listen politely to three strangers in her living room.) This all happened a little over 40 years ago—about the same time difference as the one between Jesus' public ministry and when the first Gospel (Mark) was written down.

A generation earlier, my grandparents tell the story of when my grandma went into labor with my mum. It was a cold winter's day, and my grandpa had decided to make gingerbread. Rather than making a whole tray, as he usually did, he used a muffin pan. But he didn't realize that smaller gingerbreads would cook much faster. When he got them out of the oven, they were so overcooked they were like rocks. So, he threw one at the wall, and my grandma laughed so hard she went into labor! This was over 60 years ago—around the same time difference as that between Jesus' death and when the last Gospel (John) was written. Both my grandparents remember the day.

When you think about it, the idea that people cannot possibly remember the important things that happened 35+ years ago does not make sense. If you are over 40, you probably remember significant events from your childhood. If you're over 50, you'll certainly remember things from your teenage years. We don't remember *everything* we witnessed years ago. But we retain a highlights reel of important conversations and events.

Meeting Jesus was utterly life-changing. 40, 50, or even 60 years would hardly have erased the memories. And in addition to the thousands who encountered him at various times, Jesus' disciples were trained to remember his words. Just as actors today commit vast swaths of a script to memory, so 1st-century disciples would learn their rabbi's teaching. It was their job. And in the time between Jesus' death and when the Gospels were written, Jesus' followers had taken every chance they had to share his message. Like actors staging the same play on world tour, they traveled around rehearsing their master's script.

But how do we know they weren't exaggerating?

Weren't the Stories About Jesus Exaggerated Over Time?

Earlier in the Harry Potter series, Harry's friends Ron and Hermione were both held hostage by merpeople at the bottom of a lake. Afterwards, everyone was eager to hear their tale. At first, Ron's story matched Hermione's.

But Harry "noticed that Ron's version of events changed subtly with every retelling." One week after the event, "Ron was telling a thrilling tale of kidnap in which he struggled singlehandedly against fifty heavily armed merpeople who had to beat him into submission before tying him up."[17] Richard Dawkins presents the Gospels as the result of a process like Ron's retellings, with multiple people over many years engaging in distortion and exaggeration. He imagines "early recruits to the young religion of Christianity" being "eager to pass on stories and rumors about Jesus, without checking them for truth."[18] A miracle here. A virgin birth there. And so, as the years go by, a charismatic preacher becomes divine in people's minds. But there are multiple problems with this hypothesis.

First, Jesus' most amazing miracle was his resurrection from the dead. If Dawkins' thesis is correct, we'd expect that claim to come in the later writings—like Ron's increasingly fantastical tales. But the resurrection is a major theme in the *earliest* known writings about Jesus: some of the apostle Paul's letters. What's more, if the resurrection claim had been made up by a Ron-like disciple, exaggerating for effect, there were plenty of Hermiones around to correct him. But the Gospels didn't depend on one person's testimony; instead many people claimed to have seen the risen Jesus.

Second, saying that early recruits to Christianity made up the resurrection is like saying that early

Facebook users made up social media. Without the resurrection claim, there would have been no young religion with eager new recruits! The Christian message is that God sent his Son to be born as a human, to die for our sins, and to be raised to life—so that anyone who trusts in Jesus can live with him forever. The resurrection is the engine that drives this message, not an optional extra for the luxury model. Without it, there would have been no Christian movement poised to change the world. Jesus would have been just another failed Messiah.

Third, while Ron's exaggeration of his hostage story made him more popular, the claim that Jesus rose from the dead and is now the rightful Lord of all got many of the early Christians killed. As we saw in the last chapter, Jesus' own brother James was willing to be stoned to death for proclaiming that Jesus was the resurrected King. Clearly James did not make this claim for the sake of his own reputation.

Fourth, as Dawkins himself notes, the idea that Jesus was God's promised King would have seemed "pretty bonkers" to 1st-century Jews.[19] There were plenty of freedom fighters trying to raise an army against Roman rule, and they tended to end the same way: executed on Rome's bloodiest instrument of torture. Death on a cross spelled either the end of the movement or the transfer of leadership to another candidate. Claiming that Jesus had *risen* from the dead and that people should *continue* to follow him was outrageous. Simply put, you wouldn't make this stuff up.

Which leads us to another point: rather than making the first Christians look good—and unlike Ron's story about his heroic defeat of the merpeople—the Gospels are truly terrible PR.

The Gospels Are Really (Really) Embarrassing

Close your eyes and think of your most shameful moment. (Let's do a deal: I won't tell you mine, and you don't have to tell me yours!) Now imagine that your moment of utter shame was written up in all four of the best-selling books of all time. That's what happened to the apostle Peter.

Peter was one of Jesus' closest friends. Mark's Gospel is thought to be based on his memories. If I were Peter, I'd have made sure that the write-up of my time with Jesus made me look great. But rather than airbrushing out his failures, Mark records Peter insisting to Jesus that he would never leave him (Mark 14:29) and then that same night denying three times that he even knew Jesus (Mark 14:66-72)! The other Gospels report this incident too. Ron exaggerated his story to make himself look like a hero. Peter told the story of his most cowardly moral failure. He was a major leader in the early church. The only reason he'd let this tale be told is if it was true.

And this is not the only way in which the Gospels were embarrassing.

As we saw earlier, the resurrection of Jesus is the engine driving Christianity. If I was concocting a story, I'd try to make it sound as convincing as possible. But in all four Gospels, the first witnesses of Jesus' resurrection were women. In 1st-century Jewish culture, if you had wanted a story to be believable, the last thing you'd have done was point to the testimony of women, which wouldn't have been accepted in court. Even the apostles were skeptical. When the women told them about the empty tomb, Luke writes, "Now it was Mary Magdalene and Joanna and Mary the mother of James and the other women with them who told these things to the apostles, but these words seemed to them an idle tale, and they did not believe them" (Luke 24:10-11).

This is another deeply embarrassing moment for the early Christian leaders. But the first readers of the Gospels might have had some sympathy. An outlandish tale told by a bunch of women was easily discredited. So, why did all four Gospel writers present the women as the first witnesses? It only makes sense if it's what actually happened. In fact, Bauckham argues that these women are named by Luke because they were his eyewitness sources.[20]

What About the Differences Between the Gospels?

I hope that by now you're curious enough to try reading the Gospels for yourself. I highly recommend that you do. They're the best-selling books of all time, and you could read the longest one (Luke) in the time it takes to watch a Harry Potter film! But if you read them back to back, you'll notice differences. Some stories appear in all four Gospels. Others don't. For example, only Matthew and Luke tell the story of Jesus' birth. Sometimes a story Jesus told appears in one place in one Gospel and in another place with somewhat different words in another. Sometimes different Gospels record the same events in a different order. Put all these things together and you might think that it proves we can't trust the Gospels—whether that's in what they say about Christmas or about the rest of Jesus' life. So, let's look at each of these kinds of differences in turn.

First, none of the Gospels claim to be exhaustive. John's Gospel ends, "Now there are also many other things that Jesus did. Were every one of them to be written, I suppose that the world itself could not contain the books that would be written" (John 21:25). You might think that Jesus' miraculous birth was a detail that John wouldn't want to leave out. But we'll look at the beginning of John's Gospel in chapter 4, and you'll see he chose another way to tell us that Jesus is God's Son. The four Gospels together function like a string quartet. One instrument alone can be hauntingly beautiful. But the combined effect of several instruments is yet more stunning, as each brings different treatments of the same themes into harmony.

Second, the fact that the Gospels sometimes record different sayings of Jesus in different places with different twists might at first sound fishy. But it's not. In the last few years, I've given dozens of talks in a host of different places. I often repeat material, but I mix things up for new audiences. This is standard practice for preachers, politicians, and performers even today. How much more so at a time when there was no mass media!

What about the different ordering in one Gospel versus another? It's hard to see how the order in which Jesus did things could legitimately be different in different accounts. Surely that must be a mistake. But if we think about it, we are used to storytellers not always moving chronologically. My husband, Bryan, and I recently watched the murder-mystery series *Broadchurch*. As the plot unfurled, there were multiple flashbacks. Bryan is a clever guy with a Ph.D. in engineering. But something about the precision of his brain means that flashbacks don't compute. I've learnt just to tell him when one is starting!

Why do filmmakers use flashbacks? Only to upset the engineers? No. They're inviting us to draw connections between what happened then and what is happening now. They do this in biopics too. I recently watched a film called *Hillbilly Elegy*, which is based on the memoir of a man called J. D. Vance, who is now in his thirties. It frequently wove back and forward in time. Sometimes the Gospel writers do the same thing. They order the events they record in a particular way, inviting us to make connections between the various episodes. Just as all of us (except my husband) are used to navigating flashbacks in films, so the first Gospel readers would not necessarily have expected a chronological ordering, even for a historical account.

"Ok," you might say, "so maybe the Gospel accounts of Jesus' life would pass for historical documents... if only they were recounting realistic events! But the life of Jesus that they portray is as full of would-be magic as the life of Voldemort as seen through Dumbledore's pensieve!" You're right. Rather than going around killing people, Jesus went around healing them. Rather than using the deaths of others to grasp at immortality, Jesus willingly endured death himself to give eternal life to anyone who would believe in him. But from Jesus' miraculous conception at the beginning to his resurrection at the end, his life story is full of unbelievable events. Can rational, educated 21st-century people be expected to believe in supernatural stories like a virgin birth?

CHAPTER 3

How Can You Believe in a Virgin Birth?

"I don't believe that."

I had just read my then four-year-old the account in Luke's Gospel of an angel telling Mary that the Holy Spirit was going to impregnate her with a baby who would be God's own Son (Luke 1:26-38). As there were multiple unbelievable elements in the story, I gently probed to figure out which part she didn't believe. It turned out it was the angel. She was old enough not to believe in the tooth fairy. So, surely angels were made up too!*

I got her skepticism. For many of us, the angel is the fairy on top of the Christmas tree of implausibility. A virgin birth. Wise men guided by a star. It seems the stuff of fairytales. But in this chapter, I want to suggest that these strange-sounding, supernatural claims

---

* This was the year before she told her friends that Santa wasn't real but Jesus was!

33

should not be dismissed, because if there is a God who made the universe, it's quite rational to believe the Christmas miracles. In fact, it would be irrational to discount them.

Jesus' Conception and the World's

Matthew and Luke both claim that Mary was impregnated by the Holy Spirit of God (Matthew 1:18; Luke 1:35). If this sounds unbelievable to us, it was for them as well! It took an angel showing up to convince both Mary and Joseph that a virgin could have a baby. So, who is this Holy Spirit, and how can we believe that Jesus was conceived this way? The answer to both questions lies at the very beginning.

The Holy Spirit first appears on the Bible's very first page:

> *In the beginning, God created the heavens and*
> *the earth. The earth was without form and void,*
> *and darkness was over the face of the deep. And*
> *the Spirit of God was hovering over the face of the*
> *waters. (Genesis 1:1-2)*

The Bible's first, outlandish claim is that there is one God, who created our entire universe. If this is true, then believing that Jesus was born of a virgin is not irrational. In fact, believing that God could make the whole universe out of nothing but not believing he could make one baby without a human father would be irrational. It would be like saying to someone, "I know you're an Olympic figure skater, but I bet you can't do a figure of eight!"

So, can modern, educated people really believe in a creator God?

Isn't Belief in a Creator God Outdated?

40 years ago, sociologists believed that the sands were running out on religion. As the world became more modern, more educated, and more scientific, they expected religious belief to decline. But that prophecy has failed. While religious affiliation among white Westerners has decreased in recent decades, the proportion of people across the world who say they believe in a Creator God is actually *increasing*.

Today, Christianity is the most widespread and the most racially and culturally diverse belief system in the world. About 31% of humans identify as Christian and they are roughly evenly distributed between Europe, North America, South America, and Africa—and the church in China is growing so fast that there will almost certainly be more Christians in China than in the United States by 2030, and some experts believe that China could be a majority-Christian country by 2060.[21] By then, the proportion of humans who identify as Christian is expected to increase slightly from 31% to 32%. Islam (the second-largest belief system) is expected to shoot up, from 24% to 31%. Meanwhile, the proportion of people who identify as atheist, agnostic, or just nothing in particular is set to decline by 2060 from 16% to 13%.[22]

Christianity and Islam disagree on many crucial important points. But both teach that there is one Creator God. The sands aren't running out on this belief. They're running in. Of course, the fact that most people in the world believe in something doesn't make it true. But it *does* mean that we can't dismiss belief in a Creator God as if it was outdated.

Hasn't Science Disproved Christianity?

Every summer growing up, I visited my granny. She lived in Cornwall on the edge of a beautiful bay. (If you saw the *Poldark* series, it was partly filmed in her area). Most days, we'd hit the beach. We'd build sandcastles and stand on them as the tide came in, counting how many waves they could withstand. If you read atheist authors like Richard Dawkins, you'll get the impression that when it comes to science, Christians are like kids standing on their sandcastle of faith as wave after wave of scientific discovery washes over them. The castle's gone. But they're too stubborn or deluded to admit it. Believing in science, so the story goes, is the opposite of believing in God. But this simply isn't true.

The first problem with the science-versus-Christianity story is that modern science was first developed by Christians—not despite their belief in a Creator but because of it. I learned this from Princeton Professor

Hans Halvorson, who is one of the top philosophers of science in the world.[23] The pioneers of what we now call science reasoned that if the universe was made by a rational, consistent God (as the Bible claims), then we can expect it to run according to rational, consistent laws.* But because the God of the Bible is completely free, he could have made the universe according to any laws he liked—so if we want to discover the laws that shape our universe, we need to go and look! According to Professor Halvorson, rather than being the opposite of believing in science, belief in a Creator God remains the best philosophical foundation for science today. In fact, he argues that atheism doesn't give us a philosophical basis for science at all.

Atheists tend to claim the opposite. They point out that one of the basic principles of science is to look for natural causes to explain the things we see in nature, rather than divine intervention. But, as Halvorson explains, the first modern scientists didn't exclude supernatural causes from their experiments because they believed there *were no* supernatural causes, but because they believed that *everything* was supernaturally caused! Their question wasn't "Is God working

---

* Two Franciscan friars, Roger Bacon (ca. 1214–ca. 1294) and William of Ockham (ca. 1285–ca. 1350), laid the empirical and methodological foundations for the scientific method. Francis Bacon (1561–1626) established and popularized it. Yes, two guys called Bacon did a lot of the legwork for what we now call science!

here?" but "*How* is God working here?" And because
the God of the Bible is unchanging and in charge of all
of time and space, they believed you could do the same
experiments at different times and in different places
and get the same results. What's more, the biblical claim
that God made humans *in his image* explains why we
mere mammals can understand the laws of the universe
at all. As the 17th-century pioneering astronomer
Johannes Kepler put it, "God [created us in] his own
image so that we could share in his own thoughts."[24]

This doesn't mean that Christians have always
agreed about how science and the Bible relate to each
other. Christians have been arguing about that since
at least the 4th century! At times, Christians have
strongly resisted scientific theories that turned out to
be true. (As we'll see later in this chapter, atheists have
sometimes done that too.) But if you look carefully at
every supposed science-versus-Christianity controversy
in history—from Galileo onwards—you'll find that
there were Bible-believing Christians on both sides.

Today, there are Christians at the forefront of every
scientific field. Cambridge Professor of Experimental
Physics, Russell Cowburn, is one example.

A Cambridge Professor's Journey to Faith

Russell grew up going to church, but he was far from
convinced by the stories of Jesus. In fact, as a teenager,
he thought Jesus probably wasn't even a real, historical

person. But in a gap year before starting as a student at Cambridge, Russell went to work in London. He had nothing to do his first weekend, so he tried out a local church. It turned out to be quite unlike the churches he'd grown up in. Right away he was invited to a Bible study. "It was really reading the Bible for the first time that changed everything," Russell recalls.

The group was studying John's Gospel, and Russell was stunned by one particular verse:

For God so loved the world, that he gave his only
Son, that whoever believes in him should not perish
but have eternal life. (John 3:16)

"I was so struck by the depth of God's love through Jesus' death," Russell recalls. "I wasn't shopping for a religion. It wasn't that I went out and did a careful study of all the world's thinkers and that I plumped for Jesus. It was that he found me. My faith is a relationship. And it's a relationship that I wasn't seeking."

Russell went on to study physics at Cambridge and is now a leading expert in nanotechnology, working to develop machines that are smaller than red blood cells! "Some people view faith as being one explanation of the world and science as another," Russell observes, "but I don't believe they're competing explanations; I think they're parallel explanations."

How does Russell account for miracles like Jesus' virgin birth or resurrection? He explains:

"Science is the description of how God chooses to work most of the time. But he is sovereign, and he can choose to work in any way he likes. And there are special times and places where he will behave differently—the most important one being the resurrection of Jesus. We know that dead bodies don't come back to life according to science. And yet Christianity is built on the observation that Jesus came back to life. And I'm very happy to say that at that special moment, God was acting differently."

Like Hans Halvorson, Russell points out that the fact that science works fits far better with a theistic understanding of the universe than an atheistic one. "At a philosophical level," he observes, "Christianity gives me the reason why science works. I think people sometimes overlook this. Without a Creator God, there is no reason why we should expect science to work." But much as he thinks scientific study is important, for Russell, it's not the most important thing: "Considering—in a thoughtful and serious way—the claims of Jesus is the most important thing any of us can do."

I know dozens of science professors like Russell: men and women at the forefront of research, who also believe that God created and sustains all things. Some grew up in Christian families. Others were raised in secular homes and came to follow Jesus in adulthood— for example, Francis Collins, who led the Human Genome Project and now directs the National Institute of Health in America. Rather than undermining their faith in God, they see their scientific study as part of their worship, and the scientific discoveries that grow their understanding of how God made the universe increase their wonder. One such discovery is the so-called "Big Bang."

The Virgin Birth of the Universe

The scientific theory now known as the Big Bang was proposed in the 1930s by a Belgian Roman Catholic priest called Georges Lemaître. At the time, it was strongly resisted by some atheist physicists. Honestly, I get it: the idea that the entire universe had begun as a single incredibly dense, energetic point—what Lemaître called a "cosmic egg"—seems so implausible. In fact, it was first called the Big Bang by an atheist physicist who was mocking the idea. It sounded absurd. It also sounded far too much like the biblical claim that God made the universe out of nothing. The previous scientific consensus was that the universe had always existed, and this fit more comfortably with atheism. As famous physicist Stephen Hawking observed in his best-selling book *A Brief History of Time*, "There were therefore a number of attempts to avoid the conclusion that there had been a big bang."[25] While there have certainly been times in history when Christians have resisted scientific advances, this is an example where the shoe is distinctly on the other foot!

Our knowledge of the physics of the universe has grown since Lemaître's hypothesis first hatched. One thing we have learned is that our world seems to be incredibly fine-tuned. If the fundamental laws of the universe were even fractionally different, there would be no stars, no planets, and no life. The weirdness of this has led some scientists to hypothesize that there are billions of other universes with different laws, and ours is the one that just happened to work out. From a Christian perspective, there's no problem with the idea that God made multiple universes. After all, he made billions of galaxies, and our tiny little planet is still central to his plans. But even if there *are* a practically infinite number of other universes, so that the fine-tuning of our universe is less implausible, we're still left with the question of why reality exists at all? Why is there *something* rather than *nothing*?

In his last book, Stephen Hawking claimed to have answered this question:

> *"Because there is a law like gravity, the universe can and will create itself from nothing ... Spontaneous creation is the reason there is something rather than nothing, why the universe exists, why we exist. It is not necessary to invoke God to light the blue touch paper and set the universe going."* [26]

But if we read closely, we'll see that Hawking hasn't really solved the problem of why anything exists in the first place. As agnostic physicist Paul Davies points out, Hawking's "spontaneous creation" depends on the existence of eternal, unchanging, transcendent laws "that just happen to exist and must simply be accepted as given." Davies observes that these laws "have a similar status to an unexplained, transcendent God."[27] In other words, Hawking argues that physical realities depend on eternal, non-physical realities—which is what Christians have been saying all along!

Yet there's far more to the Christian view of God than that. According to the Bible, God didn't just "light the blue touch paper" of the universe and step back, like my husband setting off fireworks for my kids on New Year's Eve. God rules the universe from first to last. He cares about the world he's made and the people he's made—about you and about me. We know this because of what we celebrate at Christmas. Jesus was born to be "Immanuel," which means "God with us" (Matthew 1:22-23). And when we contemplate that the eternal God out there—with the power to create billions of stars and planets—would become a tiny baby down here, born to live with us and die for us because he loves us, the only right response is worship.

What About the Guiding Star?

Like some scientists today, in Matthew's Gospel a group of astronomers—or "wise men"—were led to worship Jesus by a star. Along with the virgin birth, this is the other scientific challenge of the Christmas story. How exactly did this happen?

The short answer is: we don't know! Various theories have been advanced about comets, supernovas, or alignments of planets (of which we have some record in the right time frame for Jesus' birth). But as with the virgin birth, if there is a God who made the universe, it's not irrational to believe he guided wise men with a star. In fact, some of the top astronomers in the world believe in the Gospel accounts—not because of any scientific evidence about a star around that time, but because they believe in Jesus himself. Amusingly, one leading Christian astronomer who serves as Senior Project Scientist for NASA's Hubble Space Telescope, is called Jennifer Wiseman. (You can't make these things up!) But if God *did* guide 1st-century wise men with a star, it's not the most amazing thing about the Christmas story.

Jonathan Feng is a Professor of Physics and Astronomy at the University of California at Irvine. His groundbreaking research is leading us toward what might be a new fundamental force that would completely change our understanding of the universe— connecting the matter we already know about with the elusive "dark matter" that seems to make up most of the cosmos. Professor Feng knows more about astronomy than I ever will, and he points us to the wonder of Christmas like this: "What's truly amazing about the

Christian faith is the idea that the God who made the universe from quarks to galaxies also cares enough about us to be born as a human and to suffer and die to bring forgiveness and new life to broken people."

Choose Your Miracle

The story of Christmas stretched the credulity of my four-year-old. But some of the world's top scientists believe it to be true. And as we have seen, without God the very existence of reality itself is a question mark left dangling in the night sky. If Christianity is true, we can look up and wonder why the God who made the galaxies also cares for you and me (Psalm 8:3-4). But if there is no God, we can only look up and wonder if our lives have any point to them at all.

As Australian author and speaker Glen Scrivener puts it, "Christians believe in the virgin birth of Jesus. Atheists believe in the virgin birth of the universe. Choose your miracle."

CHAPTER 4

Why Does It Matter?

When you wake up, you won't even remember me.
Well, you'll remember me a little. I'll be a story in
your head.
But that's ok. We're all stories in the end.
Just make it a good one, eh? [28]

In an episode called *The Big Bang*, Doctor Who travels back in time to speak these words at the bedside of the sleeping seven-year-old Amy Pond. The adult Amy traveled with the Doctor. But the crack in her wall has finally succeeded in unraveling reality. The only way to save the world is for the Doctor to restart the universe and sacrifice himself. When he does, all the adventures he and Amy had together will be undone. So he goes back in time to say goodbye. He'll soon be just a story in her head.

So far in this book, I've argued that the story of Christmas *isn't* just a good story in our heads—it's a *true* story that happened in history. We've looked at the evidence that Jesus was a real person, that the Gospel accounts of his life weren't just made up, and that the miracles they describe haven't been disproved by science. In this last chapter, we'll ask, "What difference does it make whether the Bible's claims about Jesus are true or not?" And I'll suggest that if the story of Jesus *isn't* true—if he's just a story in some people's heads—we don't just lose the magic of Christmas; we lose everything. We lose life and meaning. Good and evil. Even you and me.

A Godless History of Humankind

In his global bestseller, *Sapiens: A Brief History of Humankind*, Israeli historian Yuval Noah Harari tells the story of humanity from the beginning. While Harari rejects the claims of Christianity, he nonetheless acknowledges its influence. In fact, he argues that our deepest moral beliefs today—for example, our beliefs in universal human rights and equality—are not self-evident truths. They're biblical beliefs. "The idea of equality is inextricably intertwined with the idea of creation," Harari explains. "If we do not believe in the Christian myths about God, creation and souls, what does it mean that all people are 'equal'?"[29]

Whether or not you believe in God, my guess is that you believe in human rights. You probably believe that racism is wrong, that women are as valuable as men, that rape is evil, and that the rich should not oppress the poor. But ask yourself this question: *why?* If there is no God, these claims aren't moral facts; they're opinions. If there is no God, then, as Harari puts it, "Homo sapiens has no natural rights, just as spiders, hyenas, and chimpanzees have no natural rights."[30]

British historian Tom Holland makes a similar point in his book *Dominion: How the Christian Revolution Remade the World* (2019). Holland stopped believing in God as a kid. He was far more drawn to Greek and Roman gods than to the crucified hero of Christianity. But after years of research, Holland has found himself drawn back to Jesus. Why? Because he's realized how many of the beliefs he holds dear actually depend on this crucified Christ. His belief in human equality and rights, equality of men and women, love for foreigners, and care for the poor, weak and marginalized are specifically *Christian* beliefs. History shows us that it was only as Christianity spread that these beliefs became generally accepted. The ancient Greeks and Romans would have laughed at them.

Jenga Block or Grenade Pin?

Even if historians agree that our moral building blocks came to us from Christianity, it's tempting to think we can keep the values we cherish while gently removing the claims about Jesus himself. Like easing out a bottom-layer Jenga block, perhaps we can build our moral tower higher without belief in God at all. But extracting Jesus from our moral structure isn't like gently sliding out a Jenga block. It's like pulling the pin on a grenade. In the resultant explosion, we don't just lose morality; our sense of meaning blows up too. As Harari explains:

"As far as we can tell from a purely scientific viewpoint, human life has absolutely no meaning. Humans are the outcome of blind evolutionary processes that operate without goal or purpose. Our actions are not part of some divine cosmic plan ... Hence any meaning that people ascribe to their lives is just a delusion." [31]

Do you believe your life is meaningless? Maybe you do. Or maybe you're immediately thinking of the things in your life that *feel* meaningful. My hunch is that deep down, none of us *want* Harari to be right. But if there is no God, then we're left with a disturbing reality: we live, and then we die, and like the billions of homo sapiens before us, we are forgotten.

In the Netflix film *The Dig*, archeologist Basil Brown excavates an extraordinary Anglo-Saxon site on Edith Pretty's land. In the course of the dig, Edith discovers that she's dying. Feeling the weight of her own mortality, the investigation into the centuries-old archaeological remains at the site leaves her in tears. She and Basil have the following exchange:

Edith: We die. We die and we decay. We don't live on.

Basil: I'm not sure I agree. From the first human handprint on a cave wall, we're part of something continuous. So, we... don't really die.

This is the kind of thing we tell ourselves to dull the pain. But in the end, Edith is right; if there is no God, we die and we decay. We don't live on. Any meaning we ascribe to our lives is just delusion—like scratching letters on the surface of a lake. What's more, atheist philosophers are increasingly arguing that our sense of individual identity itself—your sense that you are *you* and I am *me*—is a delusion too; it's simply the result of chemical processes inside our brains.

Is this the necessary conclusion from science? No. As we have seen, many leading scientists are also serious Christians. Conducting a purely scientific analysis of human life and concluding that it's meaningless is like conducting a purely scientific analysis of this book and concluding it's nothing but paper and ink. But if we remove God from the equation, Harari is right: morality and meaning, identity and human rights are "figments of our fertile imaginations."[32]

So, what is the alternative?

Light Shines in the Darkness

John's Gospel doesn't mention Jesus' birth. It starts much further back: before the birth of the universe itself. John's stunning opening presents a figure whom he calls "the Word":

> *In the beginning was the Word, and the Word was*
> *with God, and the Word was God. He was in the*
> *beginning with God. All things were made through*
> *him, and without him was not any thing made that*
> *was made. In him was life, and the life was the light*
> *of men. The light shines in the darkness, and the*
> *darkness has not overcome it. (John 1:1-3)*

This "Word" *was* God and *was with* God from the very first. And as John's story unfolds, we find that this "Word" is Jesus. God himself has been funneled into flesh: like a tornado touching down but bringing life instead of death.

The Bible teaches that there is one God in three Persons—Father, Son, and Spirit—who have always existed in perfect love together. But at a particular point in time, God the Son became a human being: Jesus Christ (John 1:17), "the only Son from the Father" (v 14). John says that Jesus is God's everlasting Word—the great story that God's been telling since before the universe hatched from its cosmic egg, the argument against a meaningless world, the light shining in the darkness.

Against the bleak midwinter of a world without God, John tells a story in which our lives are part of a cosmic plan. He goes on:

> *The true light, which gives light to everyone, was*
> *coming into the world. He was in the world, and*

the world was made through him, yet the world did
not know him. He came to his own, and his own
people did not receive him. But to all who did receive
him, who believed in his name, he gave the right to
become children of God, who were born, not of blood
nor of the will of the flesh nor of the will of man,
but of God. And the word became flesh and dwelt
among us. (John 1:9-14)

John presents Jesus as the author of the story—
and its protagonist. In Jesus, we see the playwright
stepping onto the stage. We see the God who made the
universe itself coming down to our backwater planet
so that we might become his children. But instead of
being applauded, Jesus was rejected. Instead of being
worshiped, he was executed. And this wasn't a tragic
accident. It was written into Jesus' script from the first.
But why?

The answer is the best news and the worst news we
could ever hear. You see, if there is a God who made us
and loves us, that's wonderful news. It means that our
lives *are* meaningful, that there *are* such things as good
and evil, and that justice and love will win in the end.
We're not just debris floating in a pointless cosmos. We
matter. But according to the Bible, this is also terrible
news, because it wasn't just the people of Jesus' day
who needed saving from their sins. We all need saving
from our sins and from the judgment of God that they
rightly deserve.

The Worst News

Jesus is sometimes billed as being the love-and-forgiveness antidote to the wrath-and-judgment God of the Old Testament. But if you read the Gospels, you'll find that Jesus—while positively dripping with love and forgiveness—also warned about God's judgment again and again. He said it is like fire (Luke 16:19-31) and like darkness (Matthew 22:13). Like hunger (Luke 6:25) and like terrible thirst (Luke 16:24). Like being locked out of a wonderful party (Matthew 25:1-12) and being locked into a hopeless prison (Matthew 18:34). In the Gospels, we see that Jesus is the one who takes the judgement in our place, but he's also the Judge (Matthew 25:31-46). We see he came at that first Christmas to heal the crack in the universe that runs through every human heart and home: the crack called *sin*.

Some of us are deeply aware of our sin, even if we don't use that word. If there is a God who sees our thoughts, words, and deeds, we know that's not good news for us. Frankly, we find it harder to believe that a God who knew our thoughts would love us enough to want to die for us than to believe that he would diagnose our moral failure. If that's how you feel, I'm glad. This is no self-help book to tell you that you are enough. You're not. And nor am I. But time and again in the Gospels, the people who knew they weren't good enough for God were the people Jesus welcomed. Those seen as too bad to be bothered with or too broken to be fixed were

Jesus' preferred company. When the religious leaders criticized Jesus for spending time with "sinners," he replied, "It is not the healthy who need a doctor, but the sick. I have not come to call the righteous, but sinners to repentance" (Luke 5:31-32, NIV). The religious people's problem was that they didn't realize they were sinners too.

Likewise today, while some of us would be quick to agree that we are sinners, others are not so sure. Maybe you think of yourself as basically good—not perfect, certainly, but not a sinner who deserves God's judgment. If that's your first reaction, let me ask you this: how would you feel if other people knew your thoughts?

No Filter

In one episode of *House M.D.*, the hard-bitten diagnostician Dr. House is confronted with a man called Nick. Due to a rare medical condition, Nick has lost all inhibitions; he just speaks what he thinks. His only hope of a cure is a complex operation right next to his brain stem. "The slightest mistake could kill you," House explains. "Even if you survive, you may never be able to breathe on your own again." Despite the risks, Nick wants the surgery. Why? Because constantly voicing his thoughts is ruining his life.

If I were Nick, I'd take the surgery too. Within 24 hours of speaking all my truth, all my relationships would die. Not all my thoughts are bad. But enough are (even about those I love the most) that speaking them would devastate my life. If you and I were stuck like Nick, we'd be exposed in all our selfishness, envy, meanness, and lust. The bad news is that God can see our thoughts. He sees our words and deeds as well. He sees our mistreatment of others and our deep-down, hardened rejection of him.

But is our sin that serious?

It's easy for me to think that I wouldn't be capable of something *really* bad—like murder. But the fact is, I've never been put to the test. One thing that really struck me in the *Broadchurch* series was that when the murderers are revealed, we find that none of them had really meant to kill. Things had got out of hand, and they'd killed to cover other guilt. I found this sobering to watch. It reminded me of one of Jesus' most uncomfortable teachings: that there is no bright white line between you or me and a murderer (Matthew 5:21-22). We all stand before Jesus guilty to the core. Like someone getting an unexpected cancer diagnosis, we may have thought we were morally healthy, but Jesus says we're desperately spiritually sick. This is terrible news. But it's not the end of the story.

The Doctor Dies

At a critical point in *The Big Bang*, the Doctor finds a way to save the world. He can reboot the universe. He just needs to erase himself. Time and again in the series, the Doctor makes some version of this choice. He'll sacrifice himself to save the universe. Or just a single life. The Doctor is "the man who can turn an army around at the mention of his name."[33] But he refuses to use force. He always looks out for the outsider and in 900 years of traveling through time and space, he's "never met anybody who wasn't important."[34] I love watching this fictional, brilliant, life-giving, world-saving Doctor, because he reminds me of a real one.

Jesus always welcomed the outsider. He protected the weak, healed the sick, and fed the poor. He welcomed prostitutes, touched lepers, and held infants in his arms. Although he was God's promised King, he came "not to be served but to serve, and to give his life as a ransom for many" (Matthew 20:28). The Son of God was born to die: to save his people from their sins (Matthew 1:21).

And so, about 33 years after his birth in Bethlehem, Jesus died on a cross just outside Jerusalem. On the face of it, it was the religious leaders and Roman authorities who planned to have him crucified. But Jesus planned it too. On the cross, he sacrificed himself to save us from the judgment we deserve. Jesus—the one person in history whose thoughts and words and deeds were only good—willingly took the punishment for every evil thought and word and deed that's ever gushed out of my heart or yours. But Jesus' death was not the end of the story. Three days later, his tomb was empty, and Jesus himself appeared to his followers, alive. Jesus was raised to life once and for all. He faced death to defeat it. He paid for our sins so that we wouldn't have to. He is the great Doctor, who came for those who know they're sick and gave his life to make us well. He knows our secret thoughts and deepest shame, and yet he loves us—all the way to death and back again. He is "Immanuel" or "God with us" (Matthew 1:23). And all we have to do is trust in him.

Make It a Good One

The story of Jesus is the greatest story ever told. It's also unbelievably good news. And best of all, it's true. Rather than succumbing to a delusion, joining Jesus' story is the most real thing that could ever happen to us. We don't just live and die and get forgotten. With Jesus we will live, and die, and live again in his new world. Whatever twists and turns your tale may take, however low you feel today, however bad this Christmas is—trusting Jesus as your narrator guarantees an ending more wonderfully happy than you could ever imagine. But to get there, we must stop pretending we're the hero of the story. We must admit we don't deserve a happy ending. In fact, we are the unsuspecting villain. And yet—in the most shocking twist of all—the hero of the story loves us.

I don't know if you feel deeply known and loved today. Jesus is the one person who knows you completely:

all your thoughts, your fears, your sins, your shame. And he loves you so much he gave his life for you. My favorite Christmas carol is by the 19th-century poet Christina Rossetti. Its last verse goes like this:

What can I give him, poor as I am?
If I were a shepherd, I would bring a lamb;
If I were a wise man, I would do my part;
Yet what I can I give him: give my heart.

The gift of life with Jesus comes for free. But to receive it you must give your heart.

When we receive this gift, it doesn't just change life after our death. It changes life now too. It won't solve all your problems. Like life with the Doctor, life with Jesus involves a lot of risk and suffering, being scared and running hard. But we run with joy, knowing our happy ending has already been planned by the Narrator of the universe itself. This Christmas, give Jesus the pen and see what he will do. If we are all stories in the end, make yours a good one, eh?

Endnotes

1. https://talkingjesus.org/research-from-the-course/
   (accessed March 24, 2021).

2. Bart D. Ehrman, *Did Jesus Exist? The Historical Argument for
   Jesus of Nazareth* (HarperOne, 2012), p 4.

3. Ehrman, *Did Jesus Exist?*, p 4.

4. Bart D. Ehrman, *Truth and Fiction in The Da Vinci Code*
   (Oxford University Press, 2004), p 102.

5. Josephus's *Jewish Antiquities*, written around AD 93.
   Josephus, *Antiquities* 20.200, Loeb Classical Library 456
   (Harvard University Press, 1965), p 107-109. Another
   passage in Josephus's book talks more extensively about
   Jesus, but scholars agree that this is probably a product of
   later Christian tampering, so we will ignore that for our
   purposes.

6. See e.g. Mark 6:3; Matthew 13:55; Galatians 1:19.

7. Tacitus, *Annals* 15.44. Quoted from Peter Williams's
   excellent short book, *Can We Trust the Gospels?* (Crossway,
   2018), p 20-21.

8. Quoted from Williams, *Can We Trust the Gospels?*, p 25.

9. Quoted from Williams, *Can We Trust the Gospels?*, p 26.

10. This quotation is from the 3rd-century church father
    Origen's book, *Contra Celsum*, Book 3, Chapter 44, quoted
    from Michael J. Kruger, *Christianity at the Crossroads* (IVP
    Academic, 2018), p 34-35.

11. Quoted from Williams, *Can We Trust the Gospels?*, p 26.

12. For more information on this, see "What are the four
    Gospels?" in Williams, *Can We Trust the Gospels?*, p 37-47.

13. For evidence of this, see, "Did the Gospel Authors Know Their Stuff?" in Williams, *Can We Trust the Gospels?*, p 51-86.

14. For a summary of the issues and all the potential solutions see Darrell Bock, *Luke 1:1 – 9:50* (Baker Academic, 1994), p 903-909.

15. Richard Dawkins, *Outgrowing God: A Beginner's Guide* (Random House, 2019), p 28.

16. Richard Bauckham, *Jesus and the Eyewitnesses: The Gospels as Eyewitness Testimony* (Eerdmans, 2006), p 6.

17. J. K. Rowling, *Harry Potter and the Goblet of Fire* (Scholastic Paperbacks, 2002), p 317.

18. Dawkins, *Outgrowing God*, p 25.

19. Dawkins, *Outgrowing God*, p 26.

20. When it comes to the women listed as witnesses of Jesus' resurrection in different Gospels, Bauckham writes: "The divergences among the lists have often been taken as grounds for not taking them seriously as naming eyewitnesses of the events. In fact, the opposite is the case: these divergences, properly understood, demonstrate the scrupulous care with which the Gospels present the women as witnesses." Bauckham, *Jesus and the Eyewitnesses*, p 49.

21. See Pew Research Center Global Religious Survey, 2010, cited by Eleanor Albert, "Christianity in China," Council on Foreign Relations, March 9, 2018, https://www.cfr.org/backgrounder/christianity-china (accessed March 24, 2021). See also "Prison Sentence for Pastor Shows China

Feels Threatened by Spread of Christianity, Experts Say,"
TIME, January 2, 2020, https://time.com/5757591/
wang-yi-prison-sentence-china-christianity/ (accessed
March 24, 2021).

22. See "The Future of World Religions: Population Growth
Projections, 2010–2050," Pew Research Center, April
2, 2015, http://www.pewforum.org/2015/04/02/
religious-projections-2010-2050/ and "Size and Projected
Growth of Major Religious Groups, 2015–2060," Pew
Research Center, April 3, 2017, http://www.pewforum.
org/2017/04/05/the-changing-global-religiouslandscape/
pf-04-05-2017_-projectionsupdate-00-07/ (accessed
March 24, 2021).

23. See Hans Halvorson, "Why Methodological Naturalism,"
in *The Blackwell Companion to Naturalism*, ed. Kelly James
Clark (Wiley-Blackwell, 2016).

24. Quoted from a letter from Johannes Kepler to the
Bavarian Chancellor Herwart von Hohenburg, April 9/10,
1599, Collected in Carola Baumgardt and Jamie Callan,
Johannes Kepler: Life and Letters (New York: Philosophical
Library, 1953), p 50.

25. Stephen Hawking, *A Brief History of Time* (Bantam, 1998),
p 49.

26. Stephen Hawking and Leonard Mlodinow, *The Grand
Design* (Bantam, 2010), p 180.

27. Paul Davies, "Stephen Hawking's big bang gaps," *The
Guardian*, September 4, 2010, https://www.theguardian.

com/commentisfree/belief/2010/sep/04/stephen-hawking-big-bang-gap (accessed March 24, 2021).

28. *Doctor Who*, "The Big Bang."

29. Yuval Noah Harari, *Sapiens: A Brief History of Humankind* (Harper, 2015), p 136.

30. Harari, *Sapiens*, p 111.

31. Harari, *Sapiens*, p 391.

32. Harari, *Sapiens*, p 32.

33. *Doctor Who*, "A Good Man Goes to War."

34. *Doctor Who*, "A Christmas Carol."

the good book
COMPANY

Thanks for reading this book. We hope you enjoyed it, and found it helpful.

Most people want to find answers to the big questions of life: Who are we? Why are we here? How should we live? But for many valid reasons we are often unable to find the time or the right space to think positively and carefully about them.

Perhaps you have questions that you need an answer for. Perhaps you have met Christians who have seemed unsympathetic or incomprehensible. Or maybe you are someone who has grown up believing, but need help to make things a little clearer.

At The Good Book Company, we're passionate about producing materials that help people of all ages and stages understand the heart of the Christian message, which is found in the pages of the Bible.

Whoever you are, and wherever you are at when it comes to these big questions, we hope we can help. As a publisher we want to help you look at the good book that is the Bible because we're convinced that as we meet the person who stands at its heart—Jesus Christ—we find the clearest answers to our biggest questions.

Visit our website to discover the range of books, videos and other resources we produce, or visit our partner site www.christianityexplored.org for a clear explanation of who Jesus is and why he came.

Thanks again for reading,

Your friends at The Good Book Company

thegoodbook.com | thegoodbook.co.uk
thegoodbook.com.au | thegoodbook.co.nz | thegoodbook.co.in

WWW.CHRISTIANITYEXPLORED.ORG

Our partner site is a great place to explore the Christian faith, with powerful testimonies and answers to difficult questions.